The Awakening
Echo of Love

Also by Todd Geiser

YOGASTHA SADHANA
The Comprehensive Guide to
a Modern Raja Vinyasa Yoga Practice
Hawkeye Publishers

The Awakening Echo of Love

108 Poems of Divine Union

Todd Geiser

In those quiet, sometimes hardly moving times,
when something is coming near, I want to be
with those who know secret things or else alone.

Rainer Maria Rilke

Contents

Introduction

There is a well traveled story that is told within various traditions about a wise man who, in empathizing with a youth struggling with the ways of the world, tells of having two dogs inside of him. The wise man describes one of these dogs as evil and hateful and the other dog as good and joyful. When asked by the youth which dog inside of him wins the struggle, the wise man responds, "The one I feed the most." The youth in the story plays the part of the reader of the story, as one looking for answers of how to live a happier life in the human condition of facing ongoing challenges and continual dilemmas. It is a story that provides comfort with the reminder that a choice always remains available to us regarding how we direct our energy and that none can take away the personal choice to be happy and peaceful.

A book of spiritual poetry cannot possibly deny the importance and power of finding a more harmonious daily understanding of which dog inside of us we are choosing to feed. But the teachings that come to us in support of spiritual knowledge reminds us that there is a third choice in the equation. In reading the story above, the instinct is held in our animal-like nature to identify more with the energy of the two consuming dogs as being our essential reality. However, there is another level of choosing, which the story does not raise but clearly points to in its telling, that is worth so much more in the true discovery of happiness. It is found in the wise man's declaration of the "I" as the one who feeds; an "I" that clearly is seen as one separate from either of the two dogs inside. Most certainly this story is told for the benefit of one struggling to soothe their animal-like nature in the material realm of existence. Yet it is a story that sages and mystics would most surely use to shine a light on the spiritual reality that there is a lot more going on in this life than meets the eye. Lending itself to the truth that within each of us lies the actual source of all nourishment.

How we relate to this world and how we respond mentally and emotionally to life's experiences will always be a choice - and a powerful one at that. But how we relate to ourselves prompts an understanding that draws us beyond the continuous mental and emotional fragmenting that comes from identifying with life as a consumer. This does not mean the fruits of this life are not enjoyed, they will continue to be and are meant to be. And as long as we are meeting in this world, we will likely do so over a drink or a meal. But whether feeding your belly or feeding the metaphorical good and joyful dog, this level of fulfillment will always be accompanied by hunger and an ill nature.

For the seeker on the path of spiritual fulfillment, it is necessary to recognize that the real choice in life occurs in how we come to define our sense of Self. Our individual earthly creation is based on union - the joining of female and male. An initial conception that then develops more fully only through complete unison within the mother's womb. A development that continues with necessary nurturing in our connection to those adults around us upon being born. Yet as soon as we are born, we begin to establish more fully a journey into individuality. A trajectory that culminates in a death experience that will stand as the most separating, solitary act in our life. Death needs the help of no other hand for it to occur. The grief that surrounds death proves its nature as loss and separation beyond anyone's ability to influence.

Life is lived between our beginning that is established in complete connection and belonging and this inevitable ending that reminds us of our individuality and separateness. The personal yearning to reestablish or regain our inherent connection motivates most decisions and actions taken throughout our lifetime. Whether it is finding a way to belong within the scope of family and friends; or whether it is seeking the recognition of material successes in society; or just fending off feelings of loneliness and isolation; our desire to connect seems to be a never-ending search. It is the recognition of this inherent contrast that would spark a greater desire for a connection that death itself cannot touch. A connection beyond all energetic comings and goings - a union that can only be described as divine.

A person exists because an ego exists, and it is this ego that filters all emotional experiences that spur our earthly quest for connection. Our emotions connect us to others - but with the ego at the helm, individuality is continually reaffirmed, preventing this desire for union to be truly fulfilled. There is no better word for the essence of union than love. The purest love in life is always revealed when the ego vanishes. There are moments in personal relationships where this is found; the love in another's eyes reflecting the purity of truth within. But purity is not where the ego lives, and it takes many outward turnings in life to draw us closer and closer to the understanding that the fulfillment of all desire for union is an inside job.

In spiritual sadhana, love transcends its ordinary usage as a word describing something which we would give out or receive. The word *love* is often recognized in its overuse as a romantic expression, a flippant salutation, or a peripheral patch placed over a wounded world. But the power of this word is not in what it stands for at the surface, but in the depth that it pulls one into. Love remains at the core of our existence, as the very essence of our being. Love is the word that signifies, in verb-like fashion, our source in a living God.

How much of our earthly life can be said to be spiritual or how much of the spiritual life remains as something other than the turning of time is a universal question that is only answered through the pulse of a life lived. Spiritual sadhana is a path that one does not stumble upon, but is deliberately shaped and cultivated. Discernment is the necessary tool to cut through the many obstacles, distractions, and attachments that are found in a mind that faces outward. Discernment is often depicted as a sword, in that it cuts down those choices that cause ignorance and confusion. The initial steps of wielding this sword must begin with the mindfulness of choice behind those thoughts, emotions and behaviors we feed. The height of this discernment though, is established in the very knowledge of the one who chooses in the first place; where the sword is ultimately held up that the ego may fall upon it in its surrender. A surrender of that which you are not. A return home to the unification of the timeless Self. The poems on these pages are inspired by spiritual teachings from different traditions at distant points in time, all as an echo of that single source.

Meister Eckhart

Late in the year 1327, Eckhart von Hochheim very quietly passed away; a passing so quiet in fact that the exact date remains unknown. It marked a muted end to a life that was anything but. Earlier that same year, he read publicly a statement of protest in an attempt to clear suspicions of heresy imposed upon him by the Inquisition of that time. The man who had come to be known as Meister Eckhart, given the title *Master* in the language of his German origin, had dedicated a lifetime to a personal realization of God and his teachings and sermons reflected what he found on that path.

While some have looked at Eckhart as a reformer within the Christian religion, his true inspiration was that of a mystic on a lifelong search for what it meant to mature into a life divine. It was this commitment which surely delivered him to an awareness that would inevitably breach the walls of any attempt to contain it, much less institutionalize it. In 1329, Pope John XXII condemned many statements and teachings of Eckhart's as heretical. The teachings which were suppressed mostly stood in support of man's urge to find union with God through the personal understanding of what can only be known within; and the letting go of adherence to the many distractions in this world that stand without.

As a member of the Dominican Order during the early part of the 14th Century, Eckhart held a dynamic presence in his role as a preacher of God. But this preaching was not based solely on Church doctrine of the time, as this Dominican Order was new to the scene of Christian faith and brought with it an emphasis on contemplative study, prayer and meditation. Most notably, this Order promoted a spiritual life based on finding a deeply personal relationship with God - a history of teachings and practices that produced several individuals who helped shape the movement to what is now commonly referred to as Christian mysticism.

What practices or beliefs outline mysticism is impossible to categorize, but the one teaching that remains consistent is the direct realization of God. The path to the universal must be an individual one; and yet, what is always found, regardless of tradition, is consistently depicted as the most common ground. This understanding of individual subsistence on a path relative to God's unification is the very teaching that supports the doctrine of the Christian Trinity. A teaching embedded in mystery and one which, when personally explored, defines the mystic.

While most of Eckhart's teachings come to us through his sermons, it is clear that his linguistic skills had him living among his words as a preacher while knowing their limits regarding his message. In this light, Eckhart speaks to us not so much as a preacher, linguist, theologian or philosopher - but as a poet.

THAT WHICH SUSTAINS YOU SUSTAINS ME

The timeless state of being carries
not the burden of beginning nor end.

Come now, open the eyes of thy mind
and gaze upon the hidden truth within.

Those who argue for the particulars of God
look to the obvious reality before them and
tear asunder all that can be made separate.

That which sustains you sustains me.
The pure and simple being is altogether in
all things and altogether outside all things.

God is a circle
whose center is found everywhere,
and whose circumference is nowhere.

THE MIND HAS TWO EYES

The mind has two eyes-
one that looks into time and sees the diverse
and one that holds to the source of all that comes forth.
Yet these two cannot perform their office at once.

Only when the left eye discharges
its duty toward outward things
will the right eye find its timeless focus.

Every day arrives with fresh ink on your to-do list.
The light of the morning sun does not wake you up,
but lulls you back into the sleep of illusion
of what this world expects.

Do not confuse the reviving effort of clarifying your vision
with the exhaustion of so many external endeavors.
To strengthen the vision of one eye,
simply close the lid of the other.

A DROP OF WATER

Truth sits like a drop of water,
and you, a sponge.

None is lost when contact is made,
but the form of only one is seen.

With some wringing out
you can be sure of what will re-emerge.

ALL OF YOUR WORKS ARE WORKING ON YOU

All of your works are working on you,
as the hand that reaches out
is drawn nearer into its own innocence.

The essence of all morality is inwardness-
from the intensity of will in which it springs
to the nobility of the aim in which it extends.

Love will always slip through the fingers
of one who holds it as a virtue;
for it is not a seasoning
to be sprinkled upon life.

Love is life's source,
love is life's calling,
and love is life's end.

TAKE THE HEART OF A MAN

Take the heart of a man and be sure that many deaths
will be endured before muscle and mind
are put under the yoke of awareness.

Afflictions abide in those who bargain for
the affairs of this life with spiritual currency.

Like a maturing fruit itself-
one cannot ripen into sweetness
until one passes through the sourness of youth.

EVERY GIFT OF GOD

How do you measure the intelligence
of a flower opening to sunlight?

To what can you compare the wisdom
of the very breath you breathe?

Remember, your intelligence is born
from that which is greater than it.

Use wisely this wisdom that keeps looking
to compare its genius to another.

For every gift of God makes the soul
ready to receive the incomparable.

A DOOR WITH NO THRESHOLD

Nothing hinders man so much as
assigning a place and time to God.

The mind occupied with time overlooks
the very hand which winds the clock.

If one is to know God, it is in
a moment without duration.

If one is to meet God, it is through
a door with no threshold.

IF IT IS TO BE DONE

When you claim as your own anything good,
be it life, knowledge, or power, it goes astray.

For what else did Adam do?

If he had eaten seven apples and yet claimed
nothing of his own, would he have fallen?

I have fallen a hundred times more than Adam,
each of which must be healed, as was his.

If it is to be done, the divine must be made man in me;
for as it is said, *God dwells in man that man may dwell in God.*

THAT WHICH CANNOT BE CONTAINED

The first capacity of soul is intelligence,
where what is knowable remains guarded.

As a vessel attaches to the water it holds,
comprehension and understanding merge
with whatever message pours in.

The second capacity of soul is will,
where a plunge is made possible
beyond the scope of study.

As a vessel submerged in water,
form relinquishes its own domain.

A baptism, a surrendering,
to that which cannot be contained.

THE ANSWER TO YOUR PRAYERS

The answer to your prayers is to stop praying-
for if you are able, then a prayer it is not.

A prideful pleading is a measure of mood.
In true prayer the mind ascends to God alone,
an appeal beyond weight or volume.

All wishes come and go, except for
the call of a broken heart for Grace,
the reach of wounded hands for knowledge,
the longing to touch the Holy feet of eternal love.

SIMPLY REMAIN QUIET

You must comprehend that there is something
that a settle mind can comprehend
which a distracted mind cannot.

If you cannot grasp such a thing,
simply remain quiet
and it will grasp you.

THE BOUNDLESS SEA

God surely is in this moment;
but if this moment escapes to the next,
God cannot be found there.

God surely is in this breath;
but if this breath is for the sake of survival,
God cannot be found there.

God surely is in this desire;
but if this desire holds a sundered promise,
God cannot be found there.

A drop of water does not set out
to express the boundless sea;
it holds to the limits of its own form
until it returns once again to its source,
where all that is felt is the ocean.

THE PERFECTION OF DETACHMENT

I have read the writings, ancient and modern,
of heathen philosophers and inspired prophets.

I have sought earnestly to discover the
necessary quality that gives rise to Grace.

I have scaled the mountain with no other desire
than to bask in the illumination which
only a certain altitude offers.

Signs along the ascent proved to be
the same found at the apogee-
*Fullness is only known in the
perfection of detachment.*

FURTHER THAN IT OUGHT TO GO

When this life tears at the fair net
of your soul, patch it in the
surrender of sunken knees.

To make a crooked stick straight,
it must first be bent back
further than it ought to go.

So must be done to man's own nature,
in being bent back under all things
which belong to God.

THE HIGHEST EXPRESSION OF WILL

Free will-
when it comes to freedom,
nothing matches its range.

Yet, no personal claim can be made
upon anything that is truly free.

Why wrestle with this
contradiction that reaches outward,
when you can relish in the
resolving paradox that pulls inward?

The highest expression of will
is the leaving of it to its own freedom.

ONLY IN SILENCE

Three things hinder us
from hearing the everlasting word.
The first found in flesh,
the second, the spur of mind,
the third, the thrill of time.

Free yourself from the obsession of waiting
on one moment to be stolen by the next.
Release all knowledge that precedes presence.
Abandon any touch stripped of its caress.

The hallowed word cannot be heard
by the one who always has something to say.

All that the eternal Lord teaches
is the revelation of His being,
conceived only in silence.

THE EYE WITH WHICH I SEE GOD

If my eye is to discern color,
it must itself be free of all color.

Freedom receives me in my surrender
to the hand of the Almighty,
lifting me out of myself.

The eye with which I see God
is the same with which God sees me.

LET YOUR OUTWARD WORK BE DONE

One never attains to be unaffected by external things.
Never was there a saint so great as to be
untouched by earthly movements.

Your sense of tuning-in to that which is without
makes possible all of your stirrings, but to
know the one working is the chief matter.

The sound of discordance will never be
as pleasing to your ear as the harmonic.

The sight of the disparate shall never be
as beautiful to your eye as the communion.

Let your outward work be done, but
let it not outpace your understanding
that the shape of all steps taken in this life
is returning you to the refuge of everlasting safety.

THE DOOR OF AWAKENING

When the pattern of days dominate,
loss will knock at the door of awakening.

When driven by the desires of the flesh,
wounding will open that door.

When actions reflect a higher purpose,
the light divine will bid you to enter.

When each breath is the renewal of Grace,
you will have found your home.

THE WORD OF SAINTS AND SCRIPTURE

A mediator is always necessary
when one is disputing with another.

This is the word of saints and scripture.
That which is common-
both with the higher
from which it may receive,
and with the lower
to which it may impart.

A conciliation in a reluctant world,
that you may settle your grievances with God.

INTO ITS OWN LIKENESS

Fire converts wood into its own likeness.
The stronger the wind blows,
the greater the fire grows.

By the fire understand love,
by the wind the Holy Spirit.

The hallowed hold upon the flickering flames of love
impels this life of yours to expand in its own radiance.

HAVE NO CONCERN

When nothing can disturb you, heaven is your home;
certain you shall never again be offended.

When nothing can console you, hell is known;
convinced your comfort is forever in the past.

Have no concern with your many passes
back and forth through these two gates;
even within a single day and night
and without any cause of your own.

The real trouble comes when these
two are forgotten altogether.

For then, the sojourn of the soul is lost
to the banal business of making a living.

Recognize the pull of this contrast,
and do not mistake its charity;
that you may remain roused from
the slumber of temporal tidings.

THE ETERNAL ESSENCE

Inward depth is gauged by the outward.

The power of detachment always
exceeds the power of possession;
an awareness which remains an
abstraction until it is embodied.

Within form lies the eternal essence.

To overlook what meets the eye is a deceit;
to deny the transcendent is a trifle;
to embrace one through the other
puts the hand of healing upon the door of truth.

OPEN THE DOOR TO A SANCTIFIED HEART

Everything settles into its appropriate place
and God's is that of holiness.

When you open the door to a sanctified heart,
God, of necessity, must enter.

Suffering for the sake of what is holy always holds
the one who suffers in too high of regard.

The perfection of detachment is unity-
where no inclination is held to measure the Self
above or below, nor like or unlike any other creature.

Whosoever wishes to be this or that
goes on wishing for something other.
Detachment wishes not, and is fulfilled.

THE MOST NOBLE AND GRACIOUS GIFT

The most noble and gracious gift
bestowed upon any creature
is reason and will.

A human endowment, providing that one
shall be nowhere without the other.

Confer together these two always
and let neither rise to its own command,
nor turn toward that of its own profit or end.

The capacity lifting us out of the brutality of beasts
will prove to be an equal guide into the sacred.

THE RIGHT SIDE OF YOUR HEART

How can you say that God is good?

For whatever is good can be made better;
and better can always give way to best.

If I had a God whom I could understand,
I would never hold that one to be God.

Silence all thoughts destined for the outbound
and regard that which knows the essential return.

God rests in the right side of your heart.

YOUR TIME IS NOW

When you are finally sick of your sickness
you will receive the crowning cure-
the remedy of no longer postponing your arrival.

Let go now, of this waiting for your pay day,
your big break, your reward.

Let go now, of this waiting for your love to emerge
from the future, or the past.

Let go now, of this waiting for
recognition or recompense.

Let go now, of this waiting for your
life to finally begin, or to finally end.

Let go now,
into the mastery of detachment
and embrace, acknowledge, and accept
that your time is now.

Ramakrishna

When we speak of what is written in the stars, we refer to a phenomena endowed with such significance that what is preordained is not subject to chance. The many-varied choices and uncertainty on a path within the field of karma is man's journey, not God's. A genuine foretelling of fate acknowledges that which comes forth beyond the pull of human desire, beyond the prompting of a past. The astrological reading received by the parents of an infant named Gadadhar in 1836 proved to be such a telling, with the prophecy that their child would come to be recognized as a true master on earth and whose teachings would touch spiritual seekers for generations to come. The truth of which was seen in this boy who grew into the man known as Ramakrishna.

Ramakrishna lived his life in West Bengal, India, and spent much of it in the Dakshineswar Temple in devotion to his divine mother Kali, the Hindu Goddess of protection and liberation. In the early years of life, Ramakrishna was known for his ecstatic visions and silent, extended states of absorption in Samadhi. At the time, his behavior was mostly interpreted as unsettling, erratic, or outright madness by his elders and peers. It was not until a local holy woman observed Ramakrishna's strange behavior and declared his to be a *spiritual madness*, as one whose existence functions exclusively in unity with God. With a better understanding of what drove his demeanor, Ramakrishna's passion began to be seen, understood and embraced as the embodiment of Grace, rather than just an ordinary mind's struggle to find sanity in ordinary life.

As word spread of this avatar among men, devotees came from all around and would continued to seek him out for spiritual guidance. One of his students would be given the name Vivekananda, and would eventually go on to spread the word of his master's teachings, along with the message of the ancient practices of yoga, throughout the world and particularly to the west.

During his life, Ramakrishna explored the rituals of many varied religious paths and found they all took him to the same realization of God. His devotional practices were impassioned and resolute, and mostly directed toward the deities of his Hindu upbringing: Kali, Rama, and Krishna. Yet, he acknowledged a time in his life when he continually recited the name Allah upon learning of the

Islam faith and began incorporating several Muslim practices into his daily sadhana. It was also known that once introduced to the teachings of the Bible, Ramakrishna kept a picture of Jesus in his room to which he burned daily incense as an offering of praise and devotion to the Son of God.

Ramakrishna entered into this world and offered a living example of what a life of divine union looked like. His life was a testimony to the beauty and joy of sacred devotion that transcends the earthly pull, along with the harmonious principle that underlies any and all spiritual paths.

TODAY IS A DAY LIKE ANY OTHER DAY

Today is a day like any other day-
handle your karma or it will handle you.

The more you assume of worldly things,
the more you are managed by them.

Milk and water when brought together are sure to mix;
pour the mind of milk into the water of this world
and the two will undoubtedly become one.

But churn milk into butter and it will float
in the buoyancy of its own purity.

Today is a day like any other day-
affirm the spirit of courage, faith, and love
into that which this world cannot diminish.

HAVE FAITH IN YOUR OWN FINDINGS

The master heard the debate:

One declared God could not be conceived
as possessing form, for the infinite
cannot possibly be contained.

Another insisted that they have indeed
found God in form, for every contour heralds
the hand of its shaping.

The master responded the way masters do,
offering abundance found only in clarity:
"To a devotee, He appears as a personal being.
In Samadhi, He is formless and impersonal.

Have faith in your own findings and
never for a moment doubt or deny
that God with form or God without form
are both equally true."

THE GREAT BEWILDERMENT OF THIS LIFE

There is a joyful turning to this world indeed,
though its access is perpetually appraised
only in a mind turning to God.

It is the great bewilderment of this life-
to know the Grace behind its unfolding
is to reside in that space which cannot unfold.

The eternal effort of all your worldly ambitions
gives way to the One who admits them.

The sincere scope of your every responsibility
points you back to the One who grants them.

The final fulfillment of each of your desires
leads you back to the One who sustains them.

GOD SURELY DWELLS IN ALL MANKIND

It is written that God is the water of life.

Still, some water is good for drinking
and some only fit for bathing,
while filthy water you do not dare touch.

In like manner, God surely dwells in all mankind-
the faithful and insincere,
the noble and corrupt.

You know well enough to not drink dirty water,
so why would you keep company with the wicked?

Let your love extend to the hearts of all;
but remember, to some you must
bow down from a great distance.

EVERY SOUL MUST GO INTO SOLITUDE

A jug full of tears are shed
for spouse, child, sibling and friend-
how do you not find even one day to weep for God?

Every soul must go into solitude now and then.
As a creature, your social nature is expected;
as a seeker of God, the shelter of seclusion is a must.

A young tree planted on the foot-path needs a fence
that it not be trampled upon by those that pass by.
Only then will it grow that not even an elephant will disturb it.

The seed of spiritual life needs guarding from
worldly traffic, so that its roots may deepen
and that its trunk may hearten.

THE DEEPEST MYSTERY OF GOD

When teachings of God are presented as debate,
your education is on the mind of man
rather than the truth of the Divine.

Guidance in the darkness is vital,
but only in discerning the shadow's cause.

You are the light of the world -
what you are cannot be taught.

The deepest mystery of God
is that no one can teach you about God.

BEWARE OF BLIND SPOTS

You cannot know fire without knowing its power to burn.
And none can imagine a burning power
without the image of fire.

You cannot conceive of the sun's rays
without knowing the sun.
Nor can you know of the sun without bathing in its rays.

Beware of blind spots!
Those which have you praising the Absolute Brahman
while denying its embodiment;
or those which have you carousing in eternal energy
while denying its source.

GOD SMILES ON TWO OCCASIONS

My house, my health, my learning, my wealth-
an ownership made in the world of change
gives rise to an ignorance which will not.

God smiles on two occasions:

First, when brothers draw lines down the family property
and say, "That side is yours, and this side is mine."

The second, when a patient facing death
hears the doctor say, "Do not worry, I will save you."

Let not this dense world overwhelm
the spirit of light that shines upon all.

Wood placed over a small flame will certainly smother it;
but when added to a well lit fire, it serves as fuel.

YOUR TRUE SANCTUARY

None escape the struggle of significance
bound to their Creator.
Even the atheist adheres to a label
which has been formed by God.

The journey into a restful heart
is away from the tangle of opinions,
for your true sanctuary does not
accommodate that sort of fuss.

Your story is told not for character development,
but rather to make the storyteller's acquaintance.

When the gates of heaven open,
the beholding to beliefs cease-
a revealing that proves true both ways.

UNTIL THE SILENCE OF SAMADHI IS KNOWN

The buzzing bee outside the petal of the lotus
becomes silent once united with nectar.

The empty vessel submersed in water
ceases its gurgling upon being filled.

Vain disputations are the talk of God
until the silence of Samadhi is known.

THE SIMPLE LIFE IS QUITE SIMPLE

How can actions within this world
shape a path that opens beyond it?

Your livelihood can still be met
where the ego is not made so lively,
for the simple life is quite simple.

The true lover of God will never raise
the importance of their own work
higher than the lotus feet of the Holy.

With all undertakings continue to pray,
in solitude and with tears in your eyes:

"O God, grant that my work in this world and
for this world grows less and less each day;
for I forget Thee when caught in
the net of my daily determining.

Even in my noblest of deeds I sense the
anchor of attachment. For this I ask,
keep me in Thy Presence always."

THE WAY OF LOVE

The way of love and the way of knowledge
are both equally loyal, for each ultimately
delivers the same end.

But when the door of knowledge first opens,
entry will surely come through an assertion of ego;
an ownership that will seek to proudly
put knowledge to work for you.

No one can ever make this mistake with love-
for love comes forth only when
you are employed by it.

YOUR RIGHTFUL UNION

God is like a magnet; and the
mind, a needle covered in mud.

While the shroud of selfish tendencies remain,
the needle knows not the majestic draw.

Embrace the suffering this life brings
and allow all tears to wash away that
which denies your rightful union.

THE PRINCIPLE PROBLEM

The principle problem is a
mind wired to determine
the next problem.

What seems like a good plan to
avoid danger, ensures that your
danger will never have an end.

When an elephant is washed
it quickly throws dirt back onto itself;
but when kept in a clean stall
there is no risk of repeated muddying.

Do not soil your spiritual practice
in a mind triggered for trouble.

You will give rise to all that is sacred and
holy when you stop throwing the weight
of this world upon all that you do.

A MIGHTY ROAR

A roaming flock of sheep, kindhearted and sincere,
happened upon an infant tiger, deserted and forlorn.

Making it one of their own, the cub learned to eat grass;
and when the sheep bleated, the cub was heard to bleat.

A mature tiger came upon this spiritless scene,
and watched with wonder this grass gnawing cat
until it could take no more.

Dragging the cub to a water's edge
the tiger declared, "Look here!
Compare your face with mine.
Is there any doubt you are just like me?"

At first, the sheepish response was a mere bleat;
but the unshakable, wise tiger held to the
truth found in the pure reflection.

Finally, with a mighty roar
the cub found its true voice once more;
the sound of a heart no longer forsaken.

THE HOLY SPIRIT STIRS ALL MANKIND

Wind carries the scent of sandalwood,
yet none confuse the two as one.

A breeze ferries the stench of spoilage,
while it remains innocent of what is foul.

The holy spirit stirs all mankind,
while still untouched by enchantment or heartbreak.

NOT THIS, NOT THAT

Once you acknowledge you are lost,
then you may begin to find your way.

The discernment of "Not this, not that"
confiding from the core of existence.

In the discovery of what you are not,
comes the awareness of what all of *this* and *that* is.

Variety is born of unity, and that same
unity is the goal of all variety.

THE SOURCE OF OUR ARRIVAL

In the evening, fireflies think they light the world;
but when the stars shine, their conceit is subdued.

The stars in turn think their light is the brightest;
but when the moon shines, the stars are put to shame.

The moon too believes that her light illuminates all;
but lo! dawn appears and the rising sun sets things straight.

While wealth, fame and position glimmer with worth,
the pride of worldly exploits never outshines
the radiance at the source of our arrival.

ONE SOLITARY EXAMPLE

Men always speak of Janaka, the father of Sita,
as that of a man who indulged in this world
and still obtained perfection.

Yet, in the history of mankind, having
seen billions of individuals over many
centuries which have rolled away,
there is just this
one
solitary
example.

Do not think yourself to be Janaka!

Renouncing of lust, greed, and pride
is inescapable for the truth of spirit to be known.

YOUR REASONABLE NATURE

Two men entered a mango garden;
and no sooner did the worldy-wise one
begin tallying the value of each tree.

The other, in search of sustenance, made
the owner's acquaintance and with consent
plucked from the banquet before him.

While you fancy your reasonable nature,
how does this business of tree counting ever
really satisfy your deep pangs of hunger?

THE FETTERS OF THE SOUL ARE FOUR

The fetters of the soul are four:
A heart that knows shame for deeds done,
and one holding hatred for what has come;
a mind that fears what could draw near,
and one tied to pride for what is held dear.

Use your days to remove these chains,
until that instant when freedom is gained.

Caught in captivity is Jiva,
free of all fetters is Shiva.

THE COMPANY OF GOD

Material affairs will toughen your skin
as thick and rough as an alligator.

In time, not a weapon will pierce it;
and on the contrary, will fall off harmless.

Though the same occurs with spiritual matters,
the thicker your skin, the less will sink in.

To be tough is to be in the company of men.
To be unveiled is to be in the company of God.

THE ROYAL GROUNDS

What is the use of simply sitting there
deliberating God's existence?

If you are wondering if fish are in a lake, your
answer is only found through rod, reel and line.

How unreasonable it is to remain lazily on the
shore and expect clarity to jump into your lap!

If you wish to see a King in His palace, you must
be prepared to go to the royal grounds and
pass through any and all gates to reach Him.

THREE WHO PASSED BY

A sage absorbed in the communion of
Samadhi had three who passed by:

The first, a thief, who saw him and said,
"This fellow is exhausted after a night of stealing.
I must hurry along before the police arrive."

The second, a drunkard, who saw him and said,
"This fellow has fallen, unstable from a drop too much.
I must watch my steps carefully as I move along."

Last, a seeker of God, who saw him and
without a word, sat down to rub his holy feet.

THIS IS HOW IT IS WITH GOD

The sun is over a hundred times larger than the earth;
but due to its great distance from where it is seen,
it appears no bigger than a coin found in your pocket.

This is how it is with God.

We stand very, very far away from comprehending
the infinite and mistake it to be the size of
that which we can carry around with us.

A PROPER FIRE

As flames are fashioned in the glow of embers,
none would require a definite shape
for it to be called a proper fire.

When the formless becomes endowed
in form, talk of how it should appear is
useless for one who exists in its radiance.

IF YOU WISH TO THREAD A NEEDLE

The householder said to the master,
"When my boy grows, he will marry
and take charge of the family. It is then
I shall renounce my attachments
and begin yoga practice."

At this, the master responded,
"Renouncing attachments takes practice
just as acquiring them does.
Your postponement will ensure their continuity-
for as your boy grows, your spiritual path
will then defer to your grandson's wedding."

Attachments will never find their end
through the completion of a desire.

If you wish to thread a needle,
the thread must be made pointed
and all extraneous fibers removed.
An outcome determined by
the thread, not the needle.

The Cloud of Unknowing

The inspiration behind The Cloud of Unknowing comes to us from an author who chose to remain anonymous, though its history tells us it was likely composed by a Carthusian priest living in 14th Century England. What is certainly known is the spiritual relevance it has maintained since the time of its writing. The specific intention behind its guidance came as an offering of counsel to a young student, one known by the author, who was intent on pursuing a life of God. This is a text which exists as part of a rich history of the Christian contemplative and mystical tradition; one which includes works by, among others, Thomas a Kempis, Saint Teresa of Avila, Saint John of the Cross, and Meister Eckhart.

While The Cloud of Unknowing encourages the spiritual contemplative, it is worth asking what does it mean exactly to lead a life of contemplation? Specific practices and approaches do vary from culture to culture, from theology to philosophy; but it is fair to say that a contemplative is one who feels like they do not quite belong in this world as an individual isolated being, and thus sets off on a course of discovering that which is greater than the daily version of egoic life. Yet, the contemplative is not taking a journey for the journey's sake. The stirring that arises is a stirring from within, but one that has restfulness as its lure. Saint Gregory the Great, the 6th Century Pope first elected to that position from a monastic background, described the fruits of contemplation as "resting in God." He defined the pursuit of the contemplative as "one seeking a knowledge of God, impregnated with love." A life committed to contemplation is a life of opening. One where the opening of the mind and the opening of the heart are equal and full; and where the activity of opening gives way to a realm beyond movement, where restfulness is established.

As a fundamental teaching in The Cloud of Unknowing, the *cloud* imagery is used to describe a state that is the absence of a mind's contriving – a cloud that should exist between the aspirant and God. To dwell in this cloud is to dwell in a space where it would be impossible to create God in man's own image. A knowing that goes beyond the narrowness of the mind and beyond egoic perception, would be to enter into a knowledge "impregnated with love." In this cloud, there are no assumptions behind the meaning of words like *God* and *love.* The entire text of The Cloud of Unknowing is to provoke an experience of God that goes beyond the construct of ideas and concepts and to open ourselves to the indescribable presence that has been given the name God.

The journey of the contemplative is a path of Self-discovery, where what is sought is found in the unchanging, unmoving center of being. At this level, when the word love is used, it is a feeling, but hardly an emotion. Rather, it is felt as the essence of being - the truth found in a purity of where love can have no opposite. The love we experience through personal relationship in the world may reflect what we would come to know at the core of our own being, which is why it is so longed for and so sought after in this life. But the ego's involvement in what we normally call love typically gets in the way of the restfulness found in its true purity; a debasement that holds no appeal to the contemplative.

The Cloud Of Unknowing was not written as poetry, but it does lend itself to the poet. It is the structure of language and form used to point to that which cannot be captured within those parameters. May these verses support the personal opening of both mind and heart, that God's rest be known.

EMBRACE ALL SURPRISES

Embrace all surprises life offers you.

What could be more fitting guidance
to prepare you for worlds to come?

The meaning that bubbles up from your bewilderment
is worth the forfeiting of all your half-truths.

The quest for structure is merely a partial experience
and yet you spend a lifetime securing it.
In catering to the fears of your smallness,
you give up your inheritance of boundlessness.

Pay close attention; these surprises-
what are they saying each time they speak,
whether a wild scream or a quiet whisper?

Reducing you down,
reducing you down,
beyond the contraction
of where knowledge divides.

Reducing you down,
reducing you down,
into the expansion
to where love restores.

LIFT UP YOUR HEART

Lift up your heart to the hand who has written it all,
a vulnerability that reveals what is needed most.

The saints and angels rejoice in this call and all
of humanity is saved in your heart's beckoning.

No action purifies more completely than this longing;
and each who have traveled the distance
return with a consonant clarity.

The light of life that shines casts the shadow of our fears;
while truth remains beyond all laughter and tears.

A gesture on your quest, as darkness envelopes
your initial reach; for as long as it takes, stand
in your nakedness, allow for this mystery.

Remove all veils of your devising and dance in the
space not hampered by the limits of your logic.

Do not be afraid.
For reason is not the language of love; and this
unfolding of yours, a love story it has always been.

THE KEY TO YOUR FREEDOM

From where you stand you object that a cloud
only serves to block the bit of light that shines
upon you; a declaration but of your lower nature.

The constant remembrance that you are a creature
among others with teeth and nails will blind you
in a way that no amount of light will ever fix.

And though shallow comforts may be gained in
holding to such a level, the advantage of that assembly
offers no profit whatsoever where it counts the most.

You must remember to forget.
The cloud of unknowing that rises above
is buoyed by a cloud of forgetting below.

"But I am only human," you cry,
clinging to your cage like an animal.

Stop apologizing for what makes the difference!
Your humanness is the key to your freedom.

STOP THIS FOOLISH TALK

How busy you are charged with so many things
that need to get done. Even God would need an
appointment to fit into your schedule.

Your self-imposed duties and charitable deeds do have merit;
but this world does not need done
whatever it is you are about to do.

Who is it that keeps objectifying your soul day after day?

Turn away from this very question,
and all your actions will surely
add to the mire of this world.

Come to the challenge of this inquiry,
and there is hope that your endeavors
will hold a real significance.

Know the answer,
and true action pours forth.

Then,
then we can stop this foolish talk
about all that needs to get done.

THE SEED YOU HOLD WITHIN

Let weariness not overtake you!

Beat evermore upon the cloud of mystery,
and stand strong in the longing to be
intimate with that which you cannot see.

Your turning inward is not a locality,
rather a presence that arrives only
with the blind stirring of love.

All other efforts are in vain
without this tenderness.

Don't awaken earlier,
awaken each day with love.

Don't meditate longer,
sit with the sacredness of love.

Don't pray louder,
offer your petition with love.

The splendor of your virtue shines in
the renewal of this intent; and with it,
the shadow of iniquity is cast out.

THE GIFT OF IMPERFECTION

The gift of imperfection can only be opened by the meek;
for there is no surer way to discovering who you truly are.

The unassuming eye that looks upon your sordid suffering
soon turns its gaze in perfect humility to the heavenly
blaze that has blinded even the saints and angels.

The journey to opening your heart begins by staring straight
at the coverings of fear and ignorance anchored in pride.
Only in this emptying out will you partake in your entirety.

The answers you seek are not to be found,
but to be faced.

THE TRUE LOVER

It is the plight of the true lover
that ever the more you love,
the more there is longing to love.

Give up looking for another
to handle this condition.

Hang both love and longing in the mystery of your
being; beyond the light of your reason, untouched
even by the sweetness of your affections.

Abide in the nameless arrival
that comes as a caress from within.

CARRY THESE WORDS IN YOUR HEART

In God We Trust is a motto for the muddled.

There is no trust, nor spirit, when
currency holds more sparkle
than the words it puts forth.

Yet the foolish continue to say they hold
both in their hands while ego, fear,
and worry go shopping.

An earthly abundance of necessities
will always come to the true seeker.

Still, should you wander into enduring times of need,
be assured that you will be supplied a bounty
of strength and patience that will
nourish a life no morsel could match.

Carry these words in your heart, not in your hand.

In doubt, you behold to your own wretchedness.
In faith, you behold to the worthiness of God.

THE GOSPEL OF LOVE

The gospel of love is written not for another's story
to be told, but for yours to flourish in its light.

Swallow the words of its telling whole and let them fill you.

Your cure is in taking this perfect love so
personally that the ego quivers in its immensity.

The human drama is dramatically divine -
the seeker's intention that begets a tension
which cannot be contained.

The mind and hand work together to begin the scripting
of your tale; but true authorship is found in sacrificing
your stake in survival for the claim of love.

When you give up what you own for what you are,
then will you truly know what it means to be human.

DO NOT BE PUZZLED

The seeker is complex, but truth is not.

Do not be puzzled by this -
a closed fist cannot fully open without
force from the other side of the hand.

Only the fool speaks of the interior
path as a passage without effort.
This kind of talk is from one who
has dug the shallowest of wells.

If your feet are still on barren land,
surely more digging is required!

The devout stirring of love has nothing to do with labor;
though it fuels the necessary knowing of a life that
offers more than just a reasonable amount of happiness.

It is the clinging to that which stands
between your profundity and you
which must be met with vigor, courage and faith.

A path showing the way to a happiness
that was never meant to be reasoned with.

GRACE KNOWS NO AMBITION

Grace knows no ambition.

When knocking is mistaken as opportunity,
the Host goes unrecognized at His own banquet.

Before opening the door to the
sacred, all others must be closed.

The full depth of a heart detached from depravity
has no other prayer than that of unity with God.

THE FAINT WHISPER WITHIN

Balance is a counsel in the world of men and mind;
an utterance you will not hear
from the faint whisper within.

What rises from the depth of that voice
is found only in the unceasing inquiry.

Spoon fed moderation is always the
nourishment of someone else's sensibility.

Hold no measure on the inward journey,
and let your highest aspiration bring you face
to face with that which has always aspired within you.

The only way to make a life truly interesting
is to give everything you have to piercing
that which covers the sublime.

WHAT ONLY GRACE CAN DO

It is a simple question to consider:
can you grow a flower?

You combine soil, sunlight, and seed,
and take credit for what only Grace can do.

Your greatest deceit is in forgetting the simple answer.

Not one thing in life have you ever accomplished on your own.
Truth enters only where humility makes space.

THAT WHICH NEED NOT BE IMAGINED

Imagination is a wide open field;
a wilderness which returns you over
again to your own wretchedness.

The disobedience of fantasy will never cease;
rendering bodily conceit into a spiritual thing,
or else a spiritual conceit into a bodily thing.

It is the unwavering mind withdrawn
into the illumination of Grace which sees
through these images forged and false.

Sit quietly, patiently, in the beauty
of that which need not be imagined.

PRAY WITHOUT WORDS

In my youth
my prayers were long,
full of detail, with much to say.

With age
came brevity,
simplicity in my petition.

Finally,
I have come to know
how to pray without words.

THE HEART OF ALL GOOD WORK

The heart of all good work is rooted
in the meek stirring of love.

Look for no further provocation to *Thy will be done,*
for the substance of all perfection holds
nothing that is unfinished.

The only thing needed to be done
upon this earthly mirror
is you!

While the ego declares, "Divine providence has my back,"
the master affirms, "God has my face."

WHERE THERE IS LONGING FOR LOVE

Where there is longing for love,
there is love.

Grace always beckons from upstream-
a trip no ego is strong enough to make.

When laziness makes the case for the
mystery of life, the flame withers.

The beauty of the tortured path is
revealed as the fire of expanse
feeds on that very frame as fuel.

Let it be the worker
and you but the sufferer.

Know nothing,
know nothing at all except this:
where there is longing for love,
there is love.

THE CLOSEST YOU AND I CAN EVER BE

The closest
you and I
can ever be
is as a seeker.

Space abides where there are two;
a breath shared equally with saints and angels.

The sun, moon, stars, and all the heavenly lights -
although they live above the body,
still they exist beneath the soul.

All journeys eventually surrender
to the indivisible stillness.

The closest
you and I
can ever be
is as a seeker.

For beyond the edge
of where there is another,
there is just One.

ANGELS ENVY

The angels envy you for your pain.

For it is the invisible sting in your heart
from living under the sun that spurs your
naked intent, directed unto God.

Here, He can be loved for Himself,
unfettered by your folly.

Put down your tally of virtues
less the blind love, pressed and beating
upon the sacred cloud of unknowing;
where the invisible reveals the indivisible.

In this space, talk of virtue
is an embarrassment.

In this splendor, *love thy neighbor*
becomes ridiculously redundant.

A GUST OF WIND

The pilgrimage to perfection
is a convoluted course
through the contrast of will.

If you say you have no choice, you are wrong.
If you say the choice is yours, you are mistaken.

Your voice is yours alone;
shaping your path,
touching those close.
And still, one that gets swallowed
into silence by a gust of wind.

NO ONE HAS BEEN LEFT LACKING

We are all teachers,
putting forth the very lessons
we most need to learn.

A few are masters,
guiding from a place
where no gain is necessary.

While Grace quietly pulls
the heartfelt seeker into silence,
confessing that no one
has been left lacking.

NUDGE US EVER CLOSER TO GOD

Humility in suffering is what makes us human;
for any beast will run wildly away from the unpleasing,
weltering in the wealth and wonder of this world.

Show some consideration to the trouble on the horizon
and learn to suffer ably on an earth that never
stops spinning; where a desire fulfilled, is already gone.

A world of delights is a delightful thing;
but none can measure up
to how our sorrows
nudge us ever closer to God.

THROUGH YOUR INTENSITY IS YOUR TRUTH

Through your intensity is your Truth-
for only a fearless mind will step into
the fire of an intense love; where
thinker, thought, lover, and love merge.

Hard travails, sore sightings and bitter weeping
keep most in the company of the crowd nibbling
at the surface, where the securing of fortune
is spoken of as the pinnacle of prowess.

Do not deny yourself the passion
that leads to perfect Grace;
where true consolation will come,
but only when you are sure it never will.

This is not to punish but to prepare.

If you wish to know God's resting place,
bring forth a devotion that is worthy of it.

THIS ONE WE CALL GOD

We hurry to forget what no longer pleases us
with a mind consumed by the passing of days.
We get good at it, this forgetting.

A faint remembering of something brighter
turns us away from this consumption.
We are blessed by it, this remembering.

When there has never been a forgetting,
there is no talk of remembering-
this One, we call God.

An alarm, a rousing,
or perhaps we finally have slept long enough.

Eventually we do awaken
to that which only man is capable of setting aside.

THIS CONDITION IS NOT A DISGUISE

How will you ever look past the unruly madman of the ego
when you have walked as companions for so long now?
Yet, look past you must!

When in the shadow of this trespasser, stand
up straight and stare out beyond its shoulder.
Without hesitation, let it be known to the brute
before you that something else is worth seeking.

And should frailty reign, that for the sake of your
gaze such height cannot be reached, crumple
yourself under the weight of this obstruction
and concede that you are forever done.

This condition is not a disguise -
for only the sincerity of your torment
shall melt all to water.

It will be God then,
looking past the obstruction to you.

Slowly, lifting you up.
Cherishingly, drying your eyes.

THE PATH IS YOURS

When Jesus spoke of salvation,
he used metaphors, not memoirs.

When Buddha taught the way to enlightenment,
his instruction was not his biography.

Be not confused by this conundrum.

The master teaches from the impersonal
what you must personally discover.

How long the path, is yours.
How difficult the path, is yours.
How circular the path, is yours.

What you find in the end, is not.

FINISH WHAT YOU STARTED

Finish what you started,
no matter how daring the passage.

When you reach the ocean's edge,
the only offering you can make
will be the smile of parched lips-
the most sincere face
that God has ever seen.

Kabir

As is the case with all great historical figures, the myth of that person's life becomes equally great and complex, clouding the clarity of what is biographically accurate. This is particularly true with Kabir. While the beauty of his words has held tremendous influence on Hindu and Muslim history, very little is known about this mystical sage. Details such as date of birth and method of formal training are not known. He was born in Benares, India in the early to mid 15th Century, having been brought up in a family of weavers. Being illiterate, his poetry and teachings were only spoken, with his followers referring to his powerful words as *utterances*.

While Kabir is one of the most quoted poets in India, his teachings are universal. The story is told that at his death, his Hindu and Muslim disciples were disputing over the claim of the body for cremation versus burial. During the exchange, Kabir appeared to them and instructed them to lift the burial shroud. When they did, they found a bouquet of flowers where the body had been at rest. The flowers were divided so that the Muslims could bury them, and the Hindus could commit them to fire. Even in his death he brought forth a realization that could not be contained in the formal rites of religion as defined by culture and history.

His guidance extends to every person as Kabir himself never abandoned worldly life - he was a family man as much as a contemplative. Yet, he did insist that we find greater depth to this existence of ours; one where our holiness is both known and lived. This yogic attitude follows the more common western refrain to *be in this world, but not of this world.* In this approach, the aspirant yearning to know God has what is already needed, but the mind must be in tune for the divine chord to resonate clearly.

Kabir was very much opposed to dogma associated with spiritual development, the kind of action that limits the aspirant to a process of *going through the motions* that is often evident in religious life. And as most great teachers who beckon others to a higher truth that is found beyond the structure of the time, Kabir's philosophy put him at odds with religious authorities, leading to his persecution and exile. For the latter part of his life, he traveled throughout regions of northern India with a group of his disciples until his death in 1518.

Kabir's poetry speaks directly to us with regards to our own exile, one from God. His verses set to wake us up and serve as a guide back to a life that transcends individual suffering. The teachings of those who have found release from a conditioned existence are like an oil that nurtures the flame in your own heart. With your added breath to that growing fire, it burns so brightly that you are unable to deny the light of your own being.

THIS RAVISHING FIRE

The shape of these words is drawn
from the well of the unconditioned.

The solitary thought springs forth
from an endless fountain of possibilities.

You have given up all else for your vantage point,
yet the boundless remains the birthplace of the chosen.

All fruit comes from seed and within that fruit is the seed.
With fruit consumed, the seed remains for the next harvest.

There is no lasting happiness when
the source of sweetness is not known.

Your gaze is cast out to the world focused on all this shifting-
while I look into your eyes and see the
spark that started this ravishing fire.

You ask,
"How can the infinite ever be contained in a single form?"

I ask,
"How could it not be?"

THE JOY OF WAKING HAS NO OPPOSITE

Can you make it through the day
without feeling the grip of Maya?
Or is the drama of your life just too tempting?

The soul plays in many forms, but be careful
with how serious you take your investments;
for the coin of acquisition always has two sides.

If you are living the dream life
then you must be asleep.
Remember, the joy of waking has no opposite.

O soul, save thyself from the misery and pain
that comes from a world of *mine* and *thine*.
The breath of being is throttled
by the pursuit of having.

The whole world burns in the eye that desires.
The heart rests in the I that sees.

A PILLAR OF SALT

Seek the love that set you forth;
a subtle clarity that words disguise.

Enter the space between asking and not-asking;
with each breath it is renewed.

There is no depth in the ocean of love
for the ego who refuses to get wet.

O seeker,
turn mind and body
into a pillar of salt
and dive into this
ineffable union.

THEN WE SHALL MEET AT ONCE

My hopeful one, where is it that you look for Me?

I am not held in the stones that raise the temple.
Nor am I contained in the weight of your worshiping perch.
Neither rites, nor readings, nor congregation can envelope Me.

The light that shines through stained glass
is the same that illuminates your face.

The beauty of your being remains,
even through all of your becoming.

When the seeker becomes seer- then we shall meet at once,
in a moment of time that is untouched by death.

Kabir says, "God is the breath of all being."

THE WELL OF WISDOM

The fool walks by the well of wisdom,
sacrificing vision for the dust they kick up.

At last, when water is first raised
it is used merely for a bath;
a cleverness that glistens
on the surface of the skin.

Whereas the skillful one draws the bucket
and knows well enough to drink;
a transformation that strikes at the core.

While the exalted one
peering into the depth of the well,
happily leaps in.

WHY THE SAINTS SMILE

What have you come to know in this life
that has not been measured by
seeing, hearing, smelling, tasting, or touching?

Seek that knowledge and
discover why the saints smile.

AN EXPANSION BEYOND FUR AND FEATHERS

Do you talk of evolution as if you are done?
How do you measure yourself on an unfinished scale?

Your throne, your castle, your crown, your wealth,
your position, your title, your image, your name-
all are a trick of domination,
a puffing up seen among animals.

Your genuine evolving is one beyond comparing.

Stand humble before the dance of the infinite;
a vulnerability that takes you to an
expansion beyond fur and feathers.

THE OTHER WAY AROUND

Your hunger is like that of the silkworm.
Devouring day and night, spinning its own cocoon.
A process transforming it into a moth that cannot fly.
A creature that re-emerges simply to continue the cycle.

After all of this consuming,
where is your fullness?
Day by day is wasting.

This is the religion from beginning
to end that has been declared to all-
set upon your mind the contentment
and joy that only the heart knows.

Kabir says, "Dwell in that loving space of the Seer.
A life realized beyond the need to consume."

THE UNFETTERED MELODY

Planets whirl through space with a balance conveying life.
The body coordinates a plan of precise harmony.
All of nature springs forth in perfect continuity.

Symmetry blossoms in the reflection of consciousness;
yet all returns from whence it came.
In this mystery most are lost.

The ignorant refuse to see the structure to this world;
the random mind of today ensures the suffering of tomorrow.

While the confused are carried away by this assembly;
having eaten sugar, they question
how sweetness can be explained.

The wise one sees this miraculous arrangement
and gives thanks to the Beloved for the
unfettered melody to which the heart dances.

TO ALL WHO SUFFER FROM MOTION SICKNESS

The mind has made a swing that is suspended
between the conscious and unconscious.

All hang on that swing
which never ceases its sway.

The earth and sky, the sun and moon,
and every creature under the stars-
age after age, the swing goes on.

Most are seeking delight in this motion
and for a time, some do smile.

But Kabir has seen from where this
rocking began and knows the true joy.

A sight that has made him a servant
to all who suffer from motion sickness.

WHAT WOULD YOU FIND?

If you pursued the contented mind
as much as you pursue money –
would you not have it?

If you tended to the highest truth
as much as you sought your leisure –
would it not be revealed?

Can you not see
how far your grabbing has gone
beyond the sincerity of survival?

If you took all your extraneous striving
and directed it toward God –
what would you find?

ONLY THE HEART KNOWS

The senses reach out for a security
which only the heart knows.

Be careful of relationships rooted in resources;
lest you become the guard to your own prison.

Be on the lookout of the charge to be right;
or leave behind the majestic garden of your heritage.

Be leery of the pursuit of reputation and honor;
since God has no need for networking.

Your confusion comes from gorging yourself
and then stepping on a broken scale.

Kabir says, "I will fix the scale,
but you, you must learn to fast."

THIS BODY OF YOURS

Many there are that have a stake in your life.

Father and mother say, "This is our child,"
for their own advantage they do nurture.

The husband says, "She is my wife,"
like a tiger prepared to devour its prey.

Children and kinsmen, like jackals with open
mouths, lie in wait for inheritance to be had.

Can the real relation be known when held
in the confines of such selfish desire?

From the beginning, your body
has had only three true claimants:
Fire declared, "I shall consume it."
The earth affirmed, "It will be mingled with me."
And the air proclaimed, "I shall whirl it away as dust."

All other declarations of me and mine
are just mutterings of madness.

Imagine a uniting where joy spills over
the framed edges you have built.

Kabir says, "O seeker, the gift of this life is to know
the One who takes residence in this body of yours."

WHERE WILL YOU TAKE YOUR REST?

Tell me, O swan, your ancient tale.
From what land do you come? To what shore will you go?
Where will you take your rest? And what is it that you seek?

O swan, this is a good day to take flight.
Awaken, arise, follow me!

There is a land where neither doubt, nor sorrow lay claim;
where the torment of death is no more.
No need to worry if you do not know the way
for I will gladly guide you.

You will catch the fragrant scent of joy as we near;
where "thou art I" is borne on the wind
lifting you higher and higher.

Let us depart dear swan, do not delay;
for the time to fly is now.

LISTEN TO WHAT THE STARS ARE SAYING

Looking up at the night sky, into the vastness
of space, you sit small and insignificant.

For your shrinking trivialities do not stand
a chance in the face of that holy wonder.

Set aside your troubles and
listen to what the stars are saying.

It is only in expansion that the
magnificence of light can be seen.

THE ONE WHO HAS BROUGHT US HERE

All children eventually put down their toys
and cry out for the comfort, protection,
and love that only a parent can offer.

Equally, our many seasoned distractions cannot
diffuse our deepest longing to feel the embrace
of the One who has brought us here.

THE SEEKER'S MARKETPLACE

In the evening a bird sings
and all sounds fade in the mystery of this song.
Unknown, yet familiar, with both a wanting and patience;
but when morning comes, the bird is gone.

Others speak of this bird,
yet none have seen its color or form.
Each night its voice echoes off limb and leaf;
and when morning comes, the bird is gone.

This bird does not keep business hours,
with that noise it will not compete.
Its sacred melody heard only at night;
through the offerings made at its feet.

The seeker's marketplace is where it's found,
this perfect, infinite, eternal song.
And with each rising sun, we too may sing,
by heart and all day long.

FOUND ONLY IN SILENCE

Where does your anger go when you die?
Does it dissolve like the body?
Will worms eat it for nourishment?

Grief, shame, fear, depression: if they do not
stay behind, then they will surely follow along.

Of that which you accumulate in this life, it is
said that upon death you cannot take it with you.
Kabir says, "But, you must."

The turning of the mind in this lifetime will prop up
the dense cloak of the body the next time around.

Work out your release now, while alive!

Compassion and forgiveness will offer refuge,
until you finally unshackle yourself
with the key found only in silence.

AN UNWAVERING MIND

All of your choices are a reaching for comfort;
yet, your earthly longings will never
fill the infinite space of the soul.

Let all cravings get
swallowed up by one desire-
to live freely.

You have spent your whole life
trying to return to the womb.
It is time now to grow up!

The maturing of stillness,
wisdom, and kindness
found in an unwavering mind;
opening the doorway to freedom.

THE SWEETEST MUSIC

Be vigilant O yogi,
for your blessing is your curse.
Ignorance is only possible in
a mind that is free to choose.

Be ardent O yogi,
for your curse is also your blessing.
With the proper use of tension,
you will find the sweetest music.

Both freedom and love in their highest form are one.
Few there are who have realized this.

Stay true to your path; and more than all else,
cherish that which implores you from the depths
of your being, to truly be alive in this world
every day that you are.

ASK IF YOU CAN CUT IN

If a party is thrown in your honor,
would you not seek out the host in gratitude?

Don't take your cue from those
gorging themselves at the buffet;
their hunger, when satisfied, always turns to crap.

Better to be alone than in the company of the drunk;
that conversation will quickly move to boredom.

Mingle with those dancing in the
splendor of this gathering-
and ask if you can cut in.

KEEP SINGING THE NAME OF GOD

The wise words that open your heart
where spoken by one who is no longer here.

Delay no more in this understanding!
All priceless bodies were swept away;
not one remained, and not one complained.

This is the tangible secret;
your true genius is an elevated knowledge
tempered in the confines of the nine gates.

Let not your endeavors keep you
from embodying that which you truly are.

With each breath
keep singing, keep singing,
keep singing the name of God.

THE HERITAGE THAT YOU ADVANCE

O keeper of these earthly treasures,
take heed of the heritage that you advance.

Your father, his father, his father's father,
all tended to a history of buried treasures small and large.
Yet with everything that was gathered and stored,
each one left with empty hands.

Stop your affairs with these phantoms
and see the veritable tradition at hand.

Your time here is but a moment.
And yet you spend it trying to tie a rope
around the shadow of a passing cloud.

NO INTRODUCTION IS NEEDED

When water meets water,
no introduction is needed.

As the river enters the ocean,
so my heart pours unto Thee.

A love that has always been.
A love that will always be.

THE TRUE COMMUNION

If you have not come to know the containment
of your own breath, how could you possibly
know the vastness of God?

The yogi seeks the true communion,
beyond worldly conditioning.

A daily living with the knowledge
that only that which is within the vessel
will come out at the spout.

THE BOW OF MEDITATION

O yogi, your house is on the cliff's edge.
The mind hunts its prey aiming arrows
at all selfish desires roaming the wild.

Wielding the bow of meditation,
delusion, anger, lust, and greed
are driven headlong like game.

Breath after breath, day after day, ever vigilant;
yet, still you ponder: When does this work end?
How many karmas must be burned?
When does liberation come?

Kabir replies, "Stay true! Now, take your aim
at the one doling out all these questions; for that
which pervades all is here now before your eyes."

FOR THE SELF ALONE TO KNOW

O how may I speak of the unspeakable?

If I say that my body is the chamber of the holy,
then the universe shrinks with disparity.
If I say that I do not contain the
light of all, it is a falsehood.

Both hidden and manifest;
neither revealed nor unrevealed;
it is for the Self alone to know.

A fraction of the infinite, is still infinite.

Kabir says, "Rest now in that silent,
open space of the heart
which words cannot fill."

A Note on Translations

The poems in this book are unique creations rendered from early English translations of the corresponding teachings and are not presented as direct scholarly translations. These poems are offered as a modern voice to a timeless wisdom and are in support of personal contemplation and reflection on the spiritual path.

Original Translation Sources:
Abhedananda, Swami. *The Gospel of Ramakrishna.* New York: The Vedanta Society, 1907
Field, Claud. *Meister Eckhart's Sermons.* London: H.R. Allenson, Ltd., 1907
Muller, Max. *Ramakrishna: His Life and Sayings.* London, Bombay, Calcutta, Madras: Longmans, Green & Co, 1916
Shah, Ahmad. *The Bijak of Kabir.* Hamipur, U.P. 1917
Tagore, Rabindranath. *One Hundred Poems of Kabir.* London: Macmillan and Co., Ltd., 1915
Underhill, Evelyn. *The Cloud of Unknowing.* London: John M. Watkins, 1912

Index of Poems by Title

Made in the USA
Lexington, KY
21 February 2018